TALES OF OLD

Delamere Forest

R.M.Bevan

C.C.PUBLISHING (CHESTER)

Tales of Old Delamere Forest

Copyright © C.C. Publishing

A catalogue record of this book is
available from the British Library.

ISBN 0 949001 24 4

Contents

DELAMERE FOREST

The very mention of Delamere Forest conjures up romance, mystery and intrigue, and though only a small fragment of its former size, it remains one of the last enduring links, a stepping stone into Cheshire history.

Place-names, like Hart Hill, Foxey Hill and Ottersbank, roll off the tongue to remind us of when the forest was a treasured royal game preserve. Others, like Gallowsclough and Hangingstone Hill, are relics perhaps of the harsh forest laws which ruled that a poor man's life was of less worth than the rabbit he tried to snare.

Tales of witches' covens, conflicts won and lost, poachers, villains and the devil himself have all been woven into the rich fabric of Delamere Forest over the centuries.

What bloody encounter gave its name to Battleaxe Road? Who lurked in Thieves' Moss and what dark deeds were enacted in Urchins Kitchen, or Lob Slack (the Devil's Hollow)?

The answers are lost in the mists of antiquity, maybe from as long ago as two thousand years when the Roman legions hurried through, but never conquered the great forest; or from the time of King Alfred's daughter who set up a hilltop fort to look down on the dense wooded swaythes, stretching as far as the eye could see. Today, in its entirety, Delamere Forest covers an area of 2,400 acres, but in former times it stretched upwards of sixty square miles and encompassed fifty townships, from the River Gowy to the River Weaver, from Frodsham in the west, to the outskirts of Nantwich and the village of Acton, where the last old forest tree remains, a Spanish chestnut planted a thousand years ago.

This then was the twin forest of Mara and Mondrem. The Normans christened it Forest de la Mare, 'Forest of the Lakes' and the tales told, ancient and modern, are all from the Old Forest, from the King's treasure at Beeston Castle and the greatest Cistercian abbey in the kingdom, to the legend of the Cheshire Cat and the tragedy of the House of Egerton.

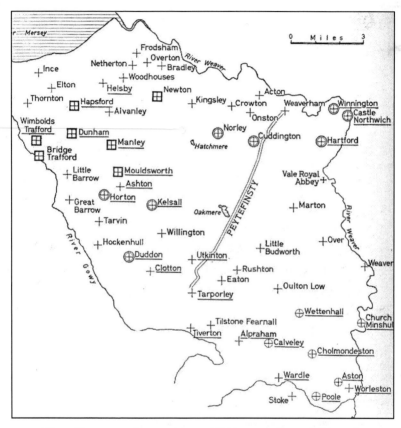

The villages and townships of Delamere Forest (Mara & Mondrem) when it stretched almost to Nantwich, from the banks of the River Mersey.

Early settlers

M an has trodden the paths of Delamere Forest from as early as the Bronze Age. Pioneering hunter-gatherers who scratched out an existence and created the first clearings. Axes have been found around Eddisbury Hill, Kelsborrow (Kelsall) and Hatchmere, and there were ancient burial grounds, 'barrows', at Seven Lows and Glead Hill Cob (Housdslow), just two of many located in and around the Old Forest.

On Eddisbury Hill, towering high above the present-day Linmere Visitor Centre, was a major Iron Age encampment. There were others along the Cheshire ridge, Maidens Castle (Bickerton), Beeston Crag, Kelsborrow Castle (Willington) and Oakmere.

However, by far the most important of these was Eddisbury and archaeological excavations have revealed that this settlement certainly survived until the Romans invaded Britain and created their legionary fortress at Deva (Chester), to accommodate upwards of 6,000 soldiers.

In order to facilitate swift and frequent troop movements, the

Eddisbury Hill and the Old Pale.

Romans built Watling Street, 500 miles from the port of Richborough (Retupiae), in Kent, via Chester to Hadrian's Wall, in the north.

Leaving Chester by the Eastgate, Watling Street partly followed an old British road and passed along the sandstone ridge at Kelsall, to enter what is now Delamere Forest, at Nettleford Wood. In the fields above Delamere School, it is said that ruts in the sandstone bedrock were possibly made by the Roman chariots of the Twentieth Legion.

From above Delamere School, the road crossed what is now Stoney Lane, skirted Eddisbury Hill and headed north towards the town of Condate (Northwich) and Manchester (Mamucium).

The Eddisbury hill-fort occupied a commanding location and the Romans perceived it as a threat to the Twentieth Legion as it marched along Watling Street. Consequently, the encampment was ransacked and the settlers ousted. After the Romans quit Britain, in the early years of the fifth century, Celtic and pagan forces dominated the so-called 'Dark Ages' and Eddisbury was resettled.

In 894, the Danes sacked Chester which was then besieged by Alfred the Great and recaptured by his son, Edward the Elder, and his daughter, Ethelflaeda, the 'Lady of the Mercians'. The Anglo Saxon Chronicles record that Ethelflaeda built a fortress, 'a city', on the site of the old Iron Age settlement at Eddisbury and here she ruled 'wisely and well'. Legend states that she called Eddisbury, 'The Happy Place'.

Eddisbury subsequently lost its place of strategic importance and yet, ironically, a thousand years later it remains a 'seat' of government, an almost empty Cheshire hilltop that lends its name to the Parliamentary constituency of central Cheshire, Eddisbury!

The line of the Roman road, above Delamere School, looking towards Kelsall and Chester. It was almost certainly an ancient British track long before the Roman invasion.

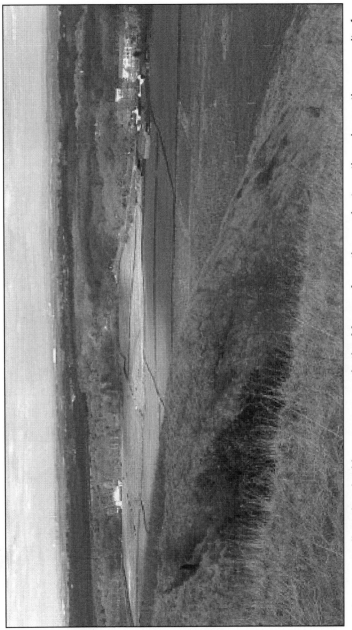

A commanding view looking west towards the Mersey from the ancient earthworks on the summit of Eddisbury Hill and the Old Pale. The land is private and the site is protected.

Master Foresters

In the 11th century, Chester was one of the last important towns to be subdued by the invading forces of William the Conqueror and much of Cheshire was laid to waste by the Normans who then ruled as feudal lords for the following two centuries. At the time of the invasion Cheshire was largely covered by the three great forests of Wirral, Macclesfield and, of course, Mara and Mondrem, i.e. Delamere Forest.

Four Norman families initially held jurisdiction over Mara and Mondrem, but in 1123 the office of Chief Forester and Hereditary Bow-bearers of Delamere was conferred, by Earl Ranulf I, on Ralph de Kingsley. The symbol of his power was a black horn which later became known as the 'Delamere Horn'.

Later, the horn and the Master Forestership descended, through marriage, to the Dones, of Utkinton, a family who went on to hold the title for almost four centuries.

The first of the line was Richard Done, 1304, who demanded many rights, some of which provide a clue to the nature of the forest in those days.

For instance, he claimed pannage, windfallen trees, wood, cropes of trees cut down and half the bark of all fallen oak. He was entitled to a halfpenny for every beast found straying in the forest, i.e. oxen, kine, bulls, heifers, bullocks and goats. Merlins, hoobies and sparrowhawks were his, as were all swarms of bees, and also the right shoulder of every deer killed.

One of the most exacting claims made was an obligation on all tenants, who held in excess of one acre of land within the forest, to provide supper, bed and breakfast for three forestry officials as they went about their business, regularly surveying the district and checking for misdemeanours.

Members of the Done family distinguished themselves in the service of the Crown at such notable engagements as the Battles of Shrewsbury and Blore Heath. Of the sixteen Dones to bear the title of Master, or Chief, Forester, four were dubbed knights, including John Done who organised the hunting for King James I during a royal visit to Cheshire in 1617.

The King so much enjoyed himself, 'hunting his own red

Sir John Done, Master Forester.

deer' in what he described as 'this delectable place', that he visited Done's house, Utkinton Hall, and there honoured his host with a knighthood.

'Arise Sir John – a gentleman very complete in many excellencies of nature, wit and ingenuity'.

During their tenure as Master Foresters, the Dones oversaw the enclosure, in the 14th century, of the 'Old Pale', to prevent the escape of deer ('pale' means 'fence'). Included within its boundaries was the Eddisbury fort site and on the 'Old Pale' a house and forest administrative centre was erected and became known as the 'Chamber in the Forest', a place locals still term a 'royal hunting lodge'. A second major enclosure, 'New Pale', occurred in the 17th century, again ostensibly to preserve 'vert and venison', though later, like the 'Old Pale', it became a farm.

Today, we see predominantly pine trees in Delamere Forest, planted and husbanded for their timber, but the old woodlands were crowded with chestnut, fir, larch, beech, oak, ash and vast numbers of silver birch. The remnants of heaths, mosses, woods and commons may still be seen, but the red and fallow deer, the otters, fulmars, ravens, choughs and kites have long since disappeared.

Delamere was, indeed, a hunters' paradise and the game, especially the deer, was jealously guarded throughout the centuries. The popular conception of a 'forest' is, quite reasonably, a large area covered with trees, dark and mysterious within; the cradle of legend and romance. But it should be remembered that 'forest' also denoted land set apart, outside the general scheme of cultivation, to form a hunting preserve for the King and his nobles, and certainly Delamere Forest, on Chester's doorstep, was a convenient 'playground' for the nobility.

The harsh and cruel forest laws of England were introduced by William the Conqueror, to ensure that all hunting and game preservation was vested exclusively in the Crown. If a man committed a felony and fled, if the lord's venison should be discovered in his house or oven, the forester and his lord divided the culprit's goods between them. His beasts and livestock, even hens and geese, his linen and woollen goods, his cooking ves-

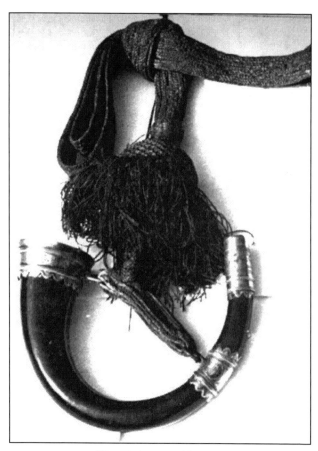

The Delamere Horn.

sels, agricultural implements, his timber, his turf and his money were at their mercy.

If a tenant trespassed or offended, the Forester could seize his estate and, if by any miracle, he was in possession of accumulated money, that would be taken as well. Under one hundred shillings and the Master Forester put the cash into his own purse; over and it went straight to the Earl. And there was short shrift for anyone caught in the act of poaching. A rope, or sword prevented further offences.

It was also illegal to carry bows and arrows in the hunting coverts, though bows might be carried on the highway, provided the strings had first been removed. The archers of Delamere Forest were some of the finest in the kingdom and were amongst King Henry V's army at the Battle of Agincourt.

The English bowman triumphed part in front
Led by the King – of Cheshire men the chief.

Generally, in the Old Forest of Delamere, it was the poor man who suffered the most, though no-one was above the law and even the Abbot of Chester was charged with trespassing and killing two deer. Only the severity of punishment differed, according to status.

The home of the Dones... Utkinton Hall still stands.

Desperate men were the foresters, desperate men were the poachers and poor men who claimed the right to 'hunt God's cattle upon God's hills'. The following, from the 'Old Brown Forest', admirably sums up the struggle:

Our King, first William, Hugh Lupus our Earl,
Then poaching, I ween, was no sport for a churl;
A noose for his neck who a snare should contrive,
Who skinn'd a dead buck was himself flay'd alive!

The forest laws were sharp and stern,
The forest blood was keen;
They lashed together for life and death
Beneath the hollies green.

This horn the grand forester wore at his side
Whene'er his liege lord chose a hunting to ride;
By Sir Ralph and his heirs for a century blown,
It passed from their lips to the mouth of a Done.

Oh then the proud falcon, unloosed from the glove,
Like her master below played the tyrant above;
While faintly, more faintly, were heard in the sky.
The silver-toned bells as she darted on high.

The metal good and the walnut wood
Did soon in flinders flee;
They tossed the orts to south and north
And grappled knee to knee.

Delamere Church, built to celebrate victory at the
Battle of Waterloo.

Continuing encroachments by cultivation began to greatly reduce the area of Delamere Forest and, in 1812, an Act of Enclosure finally brought to an end the old ways. What was left of the Forest, still a substantial acreage but a mere shadow of former days, was vested in the Crown.

The Parish of Delamere was formed and a parish church was built in 1817. This was one of the churches financed by the government and built to mark the Duke of Wellington's victory at the Battle of Waterloo. Hence, St Peter's Delamere, erected on Crown land, is still referred to as a 'Waterloo Church'.

Vale Royal Abbey

Vale Royal... a mansion was built on the site of the Cistercian
abbey, once the largest abbey church in Britain.

Timber from Delamere Forest, especially oak, was in great
demand from early times. King Edward I, the renowned
castle builder, used it to build Rhuddlan Castle, in North Wales,
whilst other large quantities went into all manner of structures,
from Chester Castle and the Mills of Dee to Northwich Bridge
and Bunbury Church. Later, seasoned timber from Delamere
was used in the construction of some of the great wooden ships
with which England ruled the waves.

However, by far the largest and most ambitious local project was the building of the great Cistercian abbey of Vale Royal, alongside the River Weaver, at what is now the village of Whitegate.

The story goes that Edward I, when Prince of Wales, escaped almost certain shipwreck on a return voyage from the Holy Lands and such was the experience that it led him to make a vow, to build the finest abbey in all England.

Edward was true to his word and vast amounts of money were channelled into the construction of Vale Royal Abbey. During one year alone, huge quantities of timber and 14,000 loads of sandstone, from the quarries at Eddisbury, were carted the five miles to the abbey site. Even glass for the windows came from Delamere Forest, made at Kingswood and remembered through the name of 'Glazier's Hollow'.

Amidst great pomp and ceremony the foundation stone was laid, on August 13th, 1277, by King Edward and his Queen, Eleanor of Castile.

The building work took all of six years and the King was present, in 1283, for the formal consecration, performed by the Bishop of Durham.

When it was finished, Vale Royal was the largest Cistercian abbey church in Britain, surpassing even Fountains Abbey, and close in size to the largest in Europe.

Vale Royal Abbey was literally carved out of the Forest of Delamere and to add to its prestige, thousands of acres of land, villages and communities fell under the jurisdiction of successive Abbots, and not always to the liking of the peasantry.

The white-robed Cistercian monks exerted great power and, often, ruled with a rod of iron against those who rebelled, or against those who did not pay sufficient homage. In total, fourteen abbots ruled Vale Royal; the most noted being the thirteenth, John Buckley who, in those days of church militants, commanded in person three hundred of the Vale Royal tenantry at Flodden.

King Henry VIII's Dissolution of the Monasteries brought an end to Vale Royal Abbey and afterwards Sir Thomas Holcroft built a great house on the site. It still stands today, now divided into residential apartments, and partly used as a clubhouse to

An old photograph showing the Abbey Arms, constructed of sandstone from Vale Royal Abbey. An inn is supposed to have stood on the site since the 12th century, at what was Pedlar's Oak.

Vale Royal Golf Club which has been created in the grounds of the ancient abbey. Can there be a more historic 19th hole anywhere in the world?

During the 18th and 19th centuries, Vale Royal was owned by the Cholmondeley family who later became the Barons of Delamere. In the early years of the 20th century, Lord Delamere, the 4th Baron, promoted settlement in Kenya and became the accepted leader of the affluent British settlers, the 'Happy Valley' set upon whom James Fox based his fascinating book, 'White Mischief', which investigated the murder, in 1941, of Lord Erroll.

The Round Lodge, at Sandiway, and the Abbey Arms, on the A556 near to the modern centre of Delamere Forest, are both constructed of sandstone removed from the Vale Royal Abbey site in the 19th century.

The curious Round Lodge, Sandiway. Legend has it that King Charles hid here, but in fact it was a gate lodge to Vale Royal.

Is there gold in them there hills?

Beeston crag, standing high and mighty, 500 feet above sea level, was part of the great Forest of Delamere when the sixth Earl of Chester set his mind to build a castle in the 13th century. Like Eddisbury, Beeston had been the site of a hill fort and settlement since the Bronze Age and there was never a more commanding site on all of the Cheshire Plain.

Beeston Castle was supposedly built on the lines of the Saracen strongholds that had given the Earl and his companions so much trouble to conquer in the Holy Land.

King Richard.

Such a desirable castle, however, soon attracted the attention of the Crown and King Henry III took possession of it, and for many years it remained a royal fortress and prison.

Legend has it that shortly before the end of his reign, King Richard II chose Beeston as a safe repository for his personal fortune of '100,000 marks in gold coin and 100,000 marks in other precious objects'.

Documentation from the 16th century suggests that some of the priceless artefacts included pieces such as a gold quadrant in a leather case, a golden reindeer lying on a green, a gold stag under a tree, a white helmet of St George, white hart brooches, cups and jewellery. Today the hoard would be worth at least £200 million !

One story claims that King Richard stored his treasure at Beeston before leaving from Chester, on an expedition to Ireland in 1399, the year of his death... and that he hid his fortune in the castle's 360ft. deep well which apparently contained a number of passages.

When Richard returned from Ireland he was taken prisoner and thrown into the gaol of Flint Castle by the forces of Henry Bolinbroke, the Duke of Lancaster, later Henry IV. The garrison at Beeston surrendered and Bolinbroke made off with the treasure. Another stab at the truth apparently surrounds old documents which were written in Norman French and point towards Holt Castle, rather than Beeston, as the resting place of Richard's treasure.

Be that as it may, many have tried to solve the mystery of Beeston Castle and if there really is treasure buried in the murky depths of the well, then not a single trace has ever surfaced, despite the use of sophisticated ultrasonic probes and magnetic detectors.

Two attempts to clear the well, in 1842 and 1935, also proved inconclusive, although the latter exploration revealed some interesting facts. The explorers found entrances to what might possibly have been three passages, but these intrepid men only reached 339ft. and they believed that there was a fourth undiscovered passage at about 350ft.

Meanwhile, Beeston Castle stands as a silent testimony to the ravages of English history, although it was not until the Civil War that it was first used in anger. Garrisoned by a Parliamentarian force, it was taken in 1643 when a Royalist captain, with eight brave men, scaled the walls at night and threw open the gates. The Governor of the Castle, Captain Steele was allowed to march, colours flying, to Nantwich with his garrison of 80 men. The Parliamentary War Council at Nantwich decided he was a traitor and the Captain was shot in Tinker's Croft, at the east end of the parish church.

Beeston Castle remained in Royalist hands for almost two years, a bitter halfway house between loyal Chester and rebel Nantwich. Finally, after a prolonged siege, the garrison was forced to surrender to Colonel Brereton.

In the 18th century, much of the castle's stonework was plundered to '... build causeways through Cheshire'. At the same time, the hill was extensively quarried. However, since 1959 the castle has been protected by English Heritage and is now open to the public on most days of the year.

The Cheshire author, Beatrice Tunstall, in her novel 'Shiny Night' (1931), wrote of Beeston as 'the old grey monarch with a castle for a crown'.

Ploughboy Prophet

For centuries, the prophecies of Robert Nixon have stirred the imagination of Cheshire folk. Supposedly born in 1467, on a small farm held by his father under the Abbey of Vale Royal, Nixon has become to Cheshire what Mother Shipton is to Yorkshire.

He was known as the 'Cheshire Ploughboy Prophet', said from his earliest years to be remarkable only for his stupidity, indeed so much so that it was with great difficulty that he was taught to drive a team of oxen, or to look after his father's cattle.

Yet he apparently became so famous that he was commanded to foretell the future for a king!

The story goes that whilst working in the fields, Nixon made many predictions, notably concerning the hamlets and villages of Delamere Forest and the Abbey of Vale Royal near where he was born, at Bark House Farm, Whitegate.

Nixon told one abbot of Vale Royal who annoyed him: 'When you the harrow come on high, Soon a raven's nest will be'. This prophecy is supposed to have come true at the Reformation when the last abbot, whose name was Harrow, was called before Sir Thomas Holcroft and put to death for refusing to acknowledge that King Henry VIII was the supreme head of the Church. Henry had given the monastery and all its lands to Sir Thomas whose crest was a raven !

Nixon is also said to have foretold the outcome of the Battle of Bosworth Field, fought between the armies of Richard III and Henry VII. Whilst ploughing in Whitegate, the simpleton stopped his team and with his whip, pointed from one hand to the other, crying 'Now Richard ! Now Harry !' several times over, until at last he said, 'Now Harry, get over that ditch and you gain the day'. The plough-holder related what had passed and the truth of the prediction was verified by special messenger sent to announce the proclamation of Henry, King of England, at Bosworth Field. Nixon, as he had foretold some years earlier, was duly sent for by the King, but upon receiving the royal command, he ran like a madman around the town of Over, declaring that at court he would be starved to death.

Upon his arrival and by way of a test, the king hid a valuable diamond ring and asked the ploughboy to help him find it, whereupon Nixon said: 'He who hideth can find'.

From then on, the King ordered that whatever Nixon said should be written down. The upshot of the tale was that Nixon, exactly as he had predicted, became locked in a closet and died of starvation. Cheshire folk said of Nixon: 'Thou were born in a forest and 'clemmed' in a court'.

Other accounts state that Nixon was born in the reign of James I (1603-25) and that he was for some time in the service of Thomas Cholmondeley, master of Vale Royal after 1625. Nixon predicted:

When an eagle shall sit on top of the house,
then an heir shall be born to the Cholmondeley family.

And so it came to pass that when an heir was most needed, a large eagle perched on the edge of a bay window and refused to be driven away until a son was born.

The Old Forest of Delamere inspired many of Nixon's prophecies and when a raven built its nest in a gargoyle at St Chad's Church, Over, it came as no surprise that soon afterwards King James II abdicated. Nixon had foretold:

When a raven shall build in a stone Lion's mouth,
on a Church top besides the Grey Forest,
Then shall a King of England be drove from his crown,
and return no more.

However, we cannot even guess as to the meaning of:

Peckforton Mill shall be removed to Luddington Hill,
and three days blood shall turn Nogginshire Mill.
A boy shall be born with three thumbs on one hand,
who shall hold three King's horses,
Whilst England three times is won, and lost in one day.

All that history tells us is that within the bounds of the Forest, a boy named Peter was born with three thumbs and lived at 'Nogginshire Mill', in the village of Cotebrook and at some time after the prediction, Sir John Crewe ordered the closure of Peckforton Mill and the removal of trade to Luddington Hill!

On firmer ground, so to speak, Nixon predicted that Norton Priory (Runcorn) would meet with Vale Royal Abbey at Acton Bridge, and this supposedly came about when the stones from the two great religious houses were used to build the bridge there.

He also spoke, maybe in the context of the Civil War, of Delamere Forest's 'Headless Cross', which can still be seen, at the side of Longstone Lane, off the A49, in Oakmere.

A Crow shall sit on the top of Headless Cross,
In the Forest so grey, and drink of the Noble's blood
gentle blood so free. Twenty Hundred horses shall want
Masters; till their girths rot under their bellies.

Nixon's remarkable visionary powers were invariably concerned with national events, some of which may have already occurred, whilst others remain unfulfilled. He told of great battles in England, one upon London Bridge and the last ever to be fought would be on Delamere Forest! Some of his other predictions were:

I must prophecy, if the favourite of a king shall be slain, the
master's neck shall be cleft in twain. (Death of Charles I)

I see men, women and children spotted like beasts, and their
nearest and dearest friends affrighted at them.
(Great Plague)

A great man shall come into England
But the son of a king
Shall take from him the victory.
The cock of the North shall be made to flee
And his feathers be plucked for his pride
That he shall almost curse the day that he was born.

The great man in this case was Bonnie Prince Charlie, and the king's son, the Duke of Cumberland, who defeated him at Culloden

... the great yellow fruit will come over to this country and flourish (King William III, Prince of Orange)

From 'mongst the dark decrees of fate,
George the son of George shall make us great.

Slaughter shall rage to such a degree,
And infants left by those that are slain,
That damsels shall with fear and glee
Cry 'Mother, Mother, here's a man!' (First World War)

Foreign Nations shall invade England with snow on their Helmets, and shall bring Plague, Famine, and Murder, in the skirts of their garments.
Three years of great wars, and in all countries great uproars, the first is terrible, the second worse,
but the third unbearable.

And asked where a man might find safety on the Day of Judgement, he said:

In God's croft, between Mersey and Dee.

Whether fact or fiction, Nixon's name and his prophecies live on to this very day, to enrich the folklore of Cheshire and Delamere Forest.

Ghosts & Legends

From ghoulies and ghosties
And long-legged beasties
And things that go
Bump in the night
Good Lord deliver us!

M agical cures and strange goings-on in the eerie shadows of Delamere Forest have long stretched the imagination of dwellers and travellers alike. And the latter, if unfortunate enough to be passing along the lonely roads and tracks after dark, were the most easily spooked.

Tales of the 'Old Witch' of Kelsall and her 'familiar', a common toad, were enough to set the blood curdling. She lived in a hovel, was regularly visited by the Devil, and the toad had once been a handsome young man who had simply knocked on her door, to ask for directions. Elsewhere in Kelsall, a woman who fell down a well is reputed to haunt Old Coach Road, whilst in Norley (the 'north clearing' of the forest) there is a legend that a ghostly form is an arbinger of death in the village.

Pagan rituals, heathen customs and witchcraft were synonymous with Delamere Forest, especially on All Hallows Eve, for this was a time when winter began and the dead roamed the skies.

A distant light from a fire in a forest clearing signalled the 'dance of the witches', when old hags in turn sprang through the blaze and a fair maiden would be barbarously sacrificed.

Perhaps that was how Maiden's Cross, an old forest mark at Alvanley Cliff, got its name!

And then there was the granite 'Devil's Thumb Stone', found on the Old Pale. Tradition has it that the Devil lived at Beeston crag and wanted to crush his adversary at Eddisbury – he missed and the stone fell into the forest!

Witchcraft, dabbling in the occult, and sorcery were black arts, an offence against the Church, and anyone out of the ordinary was viewed with trepidation and alarm. One such individual was Anna Marie Hollingworth, the 'Wise Woman of Oakmere', a stranger who appeared in a donkey cart shortly after the Napoleonic wars.

It transpired that she was travelling, with her daughter, to Liverpool, to start a new life in America. However, passing through the Old Forest she became enraptured by the solitude and sought permission to remain. This was granted and, on a piece of waste land alongside Oakmere lake, she constructed a crude dwelling, fashioned from two whale ribs which had previ-

The Old Woman of Delamere Forest.

ously been erected by Philip Egerton, of Oulton, as a souvenir of his travels. The cottage was built of turf walls and when Anna Marie's donkey died, she skinned the animal and used the hide to keep out the rain!

Superstition was rampant and at first wild stories of every kind were circulated about the poor creature who was quickly dubbed a 'witch'. In fact, Anna Marie was a charming and resourceful woman and visitors from far and wide came to visit the strange cottage and to seek her advice, and listen to tales of far away lands.

She stayed for years, constantly watching the road for her son

No longer to be seen... a figure of 'The Headless
Woman" once stood in the garden of
the inn at Duddon.

who had failed to return from the wars. One evening, a man did approach and from a distance she thought it was her son, but he never arrived. Later that night she saw men carrying a sack and dumping it into the lake. Alarmed that something dreadful had befallen her son, she alerted the authorities, and sure enough the sack was found to contain the body of a man, but not her son's body.

When her daughter married, Anna Marie 'retired' to a Dutch almshouse, in London, where she ended her days.

Ghosts were perhaps more feared than witches and Delamere Forest has always had its share.

At Blakemere Moss, many years before it was drained and planted with trees at the time of Napoleonic Wars, a coach with four horses allegedly vanished into the mire, and to this day, when the moon races from behind the clouds, it is supposed to reappear as a misty apparition.

Many a traveller has reported sighting the ghostly, galloping highwayman, near to Thieves Moss, and who knows from whence come the hooded, axe-carrying figures who allegedly frequent, Peytevinsti, the ancient Saxon highway (now, approximately, the A49) which once marked the boundary between Mara and Mondrem?

And what of 'The Headless Woman', a roadside inn at Duddon? The name is another gruesome reminder of the Civil

War when a Royalist serving wench refused to reveal, to looting Roundhead soldiers, the whereabouts of the Hockenhull family plate. She kept her mouth shut and lost her head!

Not surprisingly, there are many legends and local tales centred upon Vale Royal Abbey. A decapitated monk is said to wander the grounds, looking for his head, and the mysterious 14th century nun, Ida, is reckoned to be a permanent house guest.... a nun who made her home at a monastery!

The unfortunate monk was John Boddeworth who, in 1321, was apparently slain by the 'Olldynton' family who, to complete their dastardly deed, cut off his head and played football with it.

As to Ida, she was allegedly from Chester, or Norton Priory, and in her younger days was befriended by one Brother John, of

Ida's grave... near to where was once
Vale Royal Abbey's high altar.

38

Vale Royal, who secretly fell in love with her. Many years later, Brother John became the 5th Abbot of Vale Royal and changed his name to Peter, being more appropriate for such high office. He never forgot Ida and he was at her sickbed when she died in the convent. Her last wish was to be buried in the confines of Vale Royal, and the abbot agreed. Later, Abbot Peter was killed by rebels and Ida's soul has never been able to rest since.

Ida's grave is now surmounted by a cross in front of what is thought to have been the abbey's high altar. Inscribed on the cross is just one word - Ida.

Many people claim to have caught a fleeting glimpse of a 'dark, navy-coloured figure', or heard 'music from the heavens' at the stroke of midnight, and a medium, called to Vale Royal, says she clearly saw an image of a nun's wimple.

Tall stories? Perhaps, but not to those superstitious souls who encountered the witches and ghosts of Delamere Forest.

The Devil himself!

The old town of Over has long since disappeared from prominence, having been incorporated for several centuries into Winsford. The historian and traveller, William Webb remarked in the 17th century that 'Ouver standeth of the east end of Delamere Forest, not far from the River Weaver'.

From the 13th century, Over was a town under the jurisdiction of Vale Royal Abbey and the story goes that Over Church was literally snatched from under the noses of the monks, by the Devil!

It appears that the Devil, who had a special spite against the Abbey, tore the church from its foundations and flew off with it in his arms.

The affrighted monks alternately prayed and cursed, but failed to stop him. Suddenly, out pealed the Abbey bells and the Devil, always scared by holy music, dropped his burden.

The abbot and his monks, fearing the utter destruction of their beloved building, loudly called upon St Chad, to whom the

church was dedicated, and in answer it floated earthward, guided by the angels, 'light as the breeze-borne thistledown, as soft as a flake of snow', and landed safely on the spot where it now stands, a mile from its former site!

The Devil obviously spent a good deal of time tricking and tempting the good folk from around the precincts of Vale Royal Abbey into wicked ways. However, the proverbial shoe was on the other foot when he ran into a Franciscan friar who was taking a rest by the old stone cross at Marton.

Rather like Friar Tuck of Robin Hood legend, Friar Francis liked food and wine... in the largest quantities possible. He was just tucking into his bread and cheese, and thinking about the salmon in the River Weaver, when a voice called out:

'How's your appetite?'

It was the Devil and he wanted the friar's soul.

'Promise me whatever I want and it's yours,' responded the friar.

'Done,' said the Devil.

So Father Francis listed his three wishes. He wanted good food and wine for the rest of his life and, secondly, perfect health and good company. The Devil agreed. 'Now what's your third wish?'

'One dozen hay bands picked by yourself from Marton Sands and nowhere else,' said the wily friar who knew that hardly a blade of grass ever grew in the sandy terrain.

The upshot was that Friar Francis lived a life of contentment with an ever widening girth to prove it. He did not sell his soul and to this day the Devil is still searching for his hay bands.

The Miracle Well of Delamere Forest

A 'Miracle Well' found deep within the confines of Delamere Forest, was once said to have cured almost every known ailment, including restoring sight to the blind.

The healing powers of this magical well were described in a pamphlet, printed in London, entitled 'Newes out of Cheshire, of the Newe found Well' and followed the accidental cure of John Greenway, of Utkinton, and his three sons who were 'sick of the ague'.

It came to be known amongst the 'pilgrims' as St Stephens Well (its old established, local name was Whistlebitch Well) and upwards of two thousand of them apparently visited the spot on a daily basis to be cured of all manner of evils, either by drinking or bathing in the spa. It was claimed that the waters were effective against 'coldes, stoppings, grypings, gnawings, collicks, ulcers, blindenesse, deafnesse and nearly every other infirmity'.

Such was the excitement that the foresters had to control the crowds, to prevent inconvenience to the neighbourhood and, perhaps more importantly, to the deer of Delamere.

Referring to the former Eddisbury Hill settlement, the pamphlet stated: 'The borough or towne being utterly decaied and gone, there remaineth only upon the top of the utmost height within that situation, a proper built lodge, called the Chamber. About a mile and halfe from the Chamber towards the southwest side of the forest is the New found Well'.

Whistlebitch Well is still marked on modern maps, near to Primrose Wood, above Kelsall, and if you believe that its powers were a mere figment of faith from hundreds of years ago, consider the experience of a lady in the 1960s who had cataracts on both eyes. Within a short while of bathing them in the waters of Whistlebitch Well, the cataracts disappeared!

The Cheshire Cat

It vanished quite slowly, beginning with the end of the tail,
and ending with the grin, which remained some time
after the rest of it had gone.

L ewis Carroll, who was born Charles Lutwidge Dodgson and spent his childhood in the village of Daresbury, on the outskirts of Warrington, is generally given credit, in his tales of Alice in Wonderland, as having 'invented' the enigmatic Cheshire Cat.

But who can be sure that this puss was, in fact, crafted from the author's fertile imagination? The evidence certainly points elsewhere and amongst many theories that have been advanced, we are told that the Cheshire Cat dates from the Cornovii people who lived, during Roman times, in parts of what is now Cheshire; or that it emanates from Cheshire cheese-cloth which would sometimes contort into a grinning cat's face; or that it came from a stone grotesque representing a grinning cat, in the church at Pott Shrigley, on the eastern fringes of Cheshire; or that it is connected with Brimstage, on the Wirral.

It is quite possible, however, that the Cheshire Cat had more than a little to do with the Normans' jealously-guarded hunting preserves and particularly Delamere Forest.

In the eleventh century, the Earl of Chester was Hugh Lupus, a nephew of William the Conqueror. An enormous man he was known as Hugh 'the Wolf', or sometimes Hugh 'the Fat', and his coat of arms was a wolf's head, jaws open and teeth bared.

It was a great symbol of his authority, though, hardly surprisingly, it was despised and ridiculed by the downtrodden Saxon peasants who made their home in the Forest.

They saw not the snarl of a wolf, but the grin of a cat... a cat who had got the cream, grinning at the spoils of victory.

And so, in their eyes, 'Fat Hugh's wolf' became 'Fat Hugh's cat' and the legend of the Cheshire cat was born, long before Lewis Carroll ever thought of Alice or her Looking Glass!

Fat Hugh died without an heir and his Cheshire estates passed to his nephew, Gilbert who also inherited the family tendency to obesity. Because of it he was named 'Le Gros Veneur', the 'Fat Hunter', and from him have descended the Grosvenors who have ruled Cheshire for a thousand years.

To this day, Chester remains the family seat of the Grosvenors and the Duke of Westminster.

Who knows where the Cheshire Cat grins?

Old Man of Helsby

The Old Man of Helsby may have watched over the Mersey estuary since the beginning of time. Like a giant sentinel, Old Stone Face, the unmistakable profile of a man's face etched into the rocky escarpment, stands guard over all it surveys.

Long ago, Iron Age tribesmen built a hill fort on Helsby Tor and, in the Middle Ages, the great Forest of Delamere still reached as far as Helsby and beyond, to the marshlands of the Mersey.

The Old Man of Helsby has seen it all, the ships, the Ship Canal, the petro-chemical works, the new towns, the great Port of Liverpool, the motorways and the fearsome gibbets with their rotting corpses!

It was customary to hang an executed convict on a gibbet, on the highest hill nearest to where he had committed his crime, and so the fate of William Lownds was sealed in 1791. He would swing on Helsby Hill!

Lownds, a highway robber who specialised in stopping the

postboys and stealing their mailbags, was so notorious that he earned himself a nickname, 'The Post Master'.

On one occasion, it was said, he relieved the Chester-Frodsham postboy of his mailbags at Dunham Hill, and then fled, on horseback, one hundred miles to reach the safety of his family on Anglesey. However, as it was bound to, sooner or later, Lownds' luck ran out and after one particularly daring attack on the Chester-Warrington turnpike, he went on the run for two years until finally being apprehended in Exeter.

At Chester Assizes, and despite protesting his innocence, Lownds was found guilty and sentenced to death. On the scaffold, reported the local newspaper, he was embraced by his wife and brother and a 'sympathetic tear ran from every eye' as they took a last and long farewell.

Afterwards, Lownds' body was removed to Helsby Hill where it was hung in chains. And there, on its lofty scaffold, it remained for over five years, presently being joined by the corpses of fellow highwaymen James Price and Thomas Smallman who had also made the mistake of attacking the King's Mail. A witness who saw it all, but said nothing, was the Old Man of Helsby!

Helsby and Frodsham hills dominate the surrounding countryside and the Mersey estuary, and when the threat of invasion from the Spanish was at its height, in the 16th century, the site was part of England's early warning system.

The main threat was expected along the South coast, but it was recognised that it could be almost anywhere and the North West was considered particularly vulnerable because Ireland might be expected to support Spain.

Frodsham, with its fine, high hill was therefore a natural site for one of the warning beacons that the Elizabethans established across the length and breadth of the country.

Other safeguards were in place in case of poor visability, but in the right conditions, the chain of beacons was the 'radar' of its day and from Frodsham, the message would be conveyed along a regional chain of beacons, taking in Lancashire, Mow Cop, Shropshire and North Wales. Fortunately, and thanks to Sir Francis Drake, the invasion did not materialise and the Frodsham Beacon was never called into action.

Back in time, Hugh Lupus built a castle at Frodsham, though it was hardly as grand as the name might suggest. It was probably nothing more than a wooden structure with a tower surrounded by a palisade, with a ditch outside. During the 14th century, it was cleared and a new castle built, for the princely sum of £12. Later, the Lord of the Manor, Earl Rivers, erected a more substantial castle. The Earl was a Royalist supporter and when Parliamentarian troops seized control of the district during the Civil Wars, Frodsham Castle was 'unroofed'.

Frodsham, standing on the River Weaver, was also an important local port with a flourishing shipbuilding industry. It was a centre for Cheshire cheese and, to avoid the longer journey to Liverpool, salt from Northwich and Winsford would often be transferred from sailing flats to sea-going ships at Frodsham Bridge.

In those days though, it was all a hazardous business. In 1756, Isaac Wood, of Winsford, sent 2,750 bushells of white salt to the 'Margaretta', moored at Frodsham Bridge and bound for the Port of London. Later, passing south of the Isle of Wight, she was captured by a French privateer and the crew taken prisoner!

Cornwall clay was another commodity to pass through Frodsham. It would be unloaded and carried to the kilns of Josiah Wedgwood, while the finished crocks returned down river for onward shipping to towns and cities all over Britain.

Hunting & Racing

The swallow flies fast, but remember
The swallow with summer is gone;
What bird is there left in November
To rival the Tarporley Swan?

Horse racing and fox-hunting have been synonymous with Delamere Forest for centuries and certainly since the founding, in 1762, of the famous Tarporley Hunt Club.

At one time, Tarporley, with its own Mayor, town hall and market, was the principal 'country town' of Delamere Forest and the Swan Hotel, in High Street, proved an ideal base for the nine young sportsmen who established the hunt club.

Racing and hunting were the major pursuits of a gentleman during the 18th century and from the start they imposed strict rules upon themselves, with heavy fines for any infringement of the club's detailed costume. The original hunting costume was blue frock with plain yellow metal buttons, a scarlet velvet cape and double-breasted flannel waistcoat. This has evolved into the

The Swan - headquarters of the Tarporley Hunt Club
since 1762. To the right is the old market hall.

modern hunting dress, although Tarporley club members can
always be distinguished by their 'green collars'.

More of a social gathering these days, members continue to
meet twice yearly, in the historic Hunt Room at the Swan Hotel,
and a number still hunt the countryside around Delamere Forest,
in the tradition of the founders of the Tarporley Hunt Club. The
following was penned in 1862:

When a Swan takes to singing they say she will die,
But our Tarporley Swan proves that legend a lie;
For a hundred years past she has swung at this door,
May she swing there and sing there a thousand years more!

One of the original founders of the Tarporley Hunt Club was the wealthy George Wilbraham, of Nantwich, who purchased hundreds of acres of land around Delamere Forest, 'to be close to the fox-hunting', and to build himself a mansion, Delamere Lodge, at Cuddington.

Partly within his newly-acquired property was the old 'racecourse' at Crabtree Green (opposite to the present day 'Little Chef'), 'within the Forest of Delamere' and mentioned on maps as early as 1657, being beside 'ye carryer's road from Northwych to Chester'. Wilbraham and his co-founders of the Tarporley Hunt Club promoted an annual race meeting here and by 1809 it was listed as a permanent fixture in the official Racing Calendar.

A true and exact
Liſt of all the *H O R S E S*, &c.
That are ENTERED to run on
Crab-Tree-Green, Delamere-Foreſt, Cheſhire.
On *Tueſday* the 14th, *Wedneſday* the 15th, *Thurſday* the 16th, and *Friday* the 17th of this Inſtant *June.* 1757.

The old Blue Cap, at Sandiway.

At first the races were restricted to horses owned or nominated by Tarporley Hunt members, but in 1809 a Silver Cup was given for horses belonging to Cheshire farmers.

Later, Tarporley Races moved to other locations, one alongside the A49 at Cotebrook, 'being over the new course on Delamere Forest', and Stand House, Sadlers Lane and Racecourse Lane survive to remind us. From 1899, until the outbreak of the Second World War, a permanent course was established on the outskirts of Tarporley and it became a huge local attraction. In its heyday, after the building of the railways, thousands would flock to the course, via the railway stations at Cuddington and Beeston.

In the 19th century, Tarporley Wakes week coincided with Tarporley Races and bull-baiting, bear-baiting and cockfighting were part of the 'festivities', much to the annoyance of more genteel Tarporley folk who strongly objected to such barbaric pursuits, and the drunkenness and gambling that went with them. The bullring at Tarporley was situated in front of the Swan Hotel and the rectory gates.

Delamere Forest, with its light, sandy soil, was considered a perfect training ground for racehorses and many famous thoroughbreds emanated from here, including the winners of a Derby, two Oaks and the Grand National.

One of the most notable racehorse owners of the 19th century was Edward Geoffrey, the Lord Derby, who died in 1869. He was reputed to have won a fortune on the turf and he always maintained that it was as a youngster, whilst watching his father's horses being trained on Delamere Forest, that he developed a keen eye for a thoroughbred.

However, the most celebrated race connected with Delamere Forest involved not horses, but dogs, or foxhounds to be more precise. In 1762, John Smith Barry, a son of the fourth Earl of Barrymore, of Marbury Hall, entered into a wager for 500 guineas with Hugo Meynell, the founder of the Quorn Hunt.

At Sandiway Smith Barry kept the first pack of foxhounds in Cheshire and the bet was to resolve who owned the fastest. Smith Barry pitted his best, Blue Cap and Wanton, against Meynell's pair in a race over four miles at Newmarket. Bluecap prevailed in a few seconds over eight minutes, with Wanton a close second, and Meynell's best hound third, upwards of one hundred yards behind.

Feted as a local hero, Bluecap lived to the ripe old age of thirteen and upon his death, in 1771, a monument was erected and later the ancient Sandiway Head Inn was renamed 'Blue Cap'. The inscription on the monument, now standing fittingly at the Forest Kennels, in Sandiway, reads:

This obelisk, reader, is a monument rais'd
To a shade, though a hound, that deserves to be prais'd;
For if Life's but a stage whereupon each acts a part,
And true greatness a term that's derived from the heart,
If fame, honour and glory depend upon the deed,
Then O! Blue Cap, rare Blue Cap, we'll boast of they breed!
If no tear, yet a glass we'll pour on the brute
So high-famed as he was in the glorious pursuit.
But no more of this theme, since this life's but a race,
And Blue Cap has gone to the death of the chace.

The famous foxhound, Blue Cap.

Murder Most Foul

In 1890 the tiny villages of Alpraham and Tilstone, near Tarporley, were rocked by a sensational confession in the United States that reopened old wounds surrounding a mysterious murder in the Forest of Delamere.

The story begins in 1857, on the Tilstone Lodge estate of Edwin Corbett Esq. In the early hours of April 17th, Corbett's gamekeeper, John Bebbington, rose from his bed to make his rounds of the woods and pheasant preserves.

Nothing was heard of him again and later he was found lying dead in a ditch, with his loaded gun beside him.

In an adjacent field, the police discovered two sets of footprints – one belonging to the gamekeeper and the other set they traced to John Blagg, 47, a shoemaker and notorious poacher who lived with his wife and four-year-old child in a nearby cottage.

Blagg was a loner, some said morose, and he would sit for hours at the Traveller's Rest pub, without speaking a word to anyone. He was known to have a grudge against Edwin Corbett and had once threatened to kill Bebbington if he ever tried to take his gun away from him.

At Blagg's home, the police found a gun and cartridges similar to the one that shot Bebbington. They also found the boots, with a distinctive nail pattern, that had made the second set of footprints. As far as the police were concerned, it was an open and shut case and the pair of boots was the clinching evidence.

The trial of John Blagg took place at Chester Castle and several witnesses testified that they had seen him at the material time, in the vicinity of where Bebbington's body was found. However, crucially, at least as far as the defence counsel was concerned, they had not seen Blagg with a rifle. This was dismissed by the prosecution who maintained he could have 'broken' the weapon and hidden it in his poacher's pockets.

Throughout, Blagg protested his innocence and his counsel argued that all the evidence was circumstantial. 'The poor man is a victim of hatred because he was a poacher; and as the prosecution could not get hold of the real murderer, they pounced on the prisoner because he happened, unfortunately, to be disliked by a Cheshire country gentleman.'

Counsel also contended that though it had been established that Bebbington had been killed by an Eley-manufactured cartridge, the police had failed to find any such make in Blagg's possession.

After a trial lasting ten hours, the jury took just twenty-five minutes to find Blagg guilty and he was sentenced to be hanged.

Numerous appeals for clemency were made to the Home Secretary, but to no avail, and the word on the street was that the manorial landowner, James Tollemache, a Member of Parliament, had spoken personally and privately to the Home Secretary, and tilted the balance against the condemned man. After a visit from his wife and child, Blagg was hanged and the local newspaper reported that 'he met his death with courage and dignity'.

To the end he said it was all a parcel of lies. He maintained his story on the gallows... 'they were my boots but not worn by me!' and certainly, the Deputy Sheriff of Chester shared the widespread uneasiness. Following the execution, he said that Blagg had told him that the evidence had been falsified and the boots had been worn by someone else.

And so there the matter lay until over thirty years later, when a Liverpool merchant, James Sawers, from Neston, paid a visit to New Orleans. Here he received news of a startling confession made to the Rector of St Paul's, New Orleans. It concerned the murder of a gamekeeper, John Bebbington, in the Forest of Delamere, in 1857.

The story had come from one Henry Edwin Jones, formerly of Cheshire, who claimed to have done for Bebbington. He said, on the day before the murder, Blagg had loaned him the pair of boots that had left the tell-tale footprints. What he did not appear to explain was his motive and one assumes that Bebbington must have caught him in the act of poaching.

Jones said he had been educated at the King's School, Chester, but a sceptical Mr Sawers could find no record of him there and considered that the entire confession was all a hoax.

However, journalists who checked the story found Jones in possession of many startling minor recollections which suggested he must have been implicated, and also that he had left for America soon after the murder.

Blagg's widow, who still lived in Alpraham, confirmed that the night before the murder, Jones, who was known to her husband, had called at the cottage. He had borrowed the boots, but she could not say how or when they were returned, i.e. between the murder and the police searching the cottage. She was adamant, however, that the police had spoken with Jones but had let him go. They 'had it in' for her husband, she said.

Whether the wrong man was hanged is a matter of conjecture, but the authorities certainly did not take Jones' confession seriously. The last, tantalising, words went to Blagg's widow:

'He said if he disclosed everything that he knew he would be transported for life, and he would prefer instant death to that.'

*****

A modern murder, or to be precise a 'triple murder', stunned people living at the heart of Delamere Forest in July, 1971, when early-morning workers made a gruesome find, near to the village of Mouldsworth.

Three French campers, Daniel Berland, aged 20, and sisters Claudine and Monique Liebert had all been brutally shot where they had innocently pitched their tent on the previous evening. Daniel and Claudine were already dead, and Monique died on the operating table at Chester Royal Infirmary.

All three were from St Medard des Pres, in the tobacco-growing district of Western France, and they had arrived in the UK a week earlier, for a touring holiday in their Citroen 2CV car.

A diary, written by Monique, detailed their journey and her final entry referred to the friends being in Machynlleth, Montgomeryshire.

Piecing together other details, the police established that they had then travelled to Cheshire, via North Wales. Later they announced that a .22 rifle, stolen from a fairground in Rhyl, had been used to pump more than a dozen shots into the naked bodies of the campers.

A man living a hundred yards from the murder scene reported being awoken by 'metallic pinging' at about 2am, and looking out to see a light-coloured car parked on the roadside next to the tent.

A massive murder hunt ensued and a television appeal for information on the whereabouts of a Morris 1000 car, also taken from Rhyl, brought immediate results.

Soon the net was closing on lonely bachelor, 24-year-old Michael Bassett, who hailed from the Potteries' district of Barlaston. Fingerprints at the scene, and a torn-up letter, had placed him firmly in the vicinity of the little campsite, just half a mile from the forest road, running between Hatchmere and Mouldsworth, known locally as the 'Switchback'.

When the police got to Bassett, he too was dead, slumped in the front seat of his car, having taken his own life. Lying across his knee was an evening newspaper and eight rounds of .22 ammunition. On a .22 rifle he had scratched: 'This is the rifle with which I shot and killed three French campers at Mouldsworth, Cheshire on July 12. Signed Mick Bassett'.

Det. Chief Supt. Arthur Benfield, who led the murder hunt, said he thought Bassett had come across the campers by accident. 'Why he walked in and shot them will remain a mystery,' he added.

Villagers had their own theory. Bassett had been drinking in the local pub and had purchased a flagon of cider which he must have consumed in the lonely lay-by across from the campsite. Did he make advances on the girls and when they were spurned, did he turn to the rifle in drunken fury?

The Hangman &
The Elopement

O
ne of the principal villages in the Forest of Delamere was Weaverham, close by the River Weaver crossing on the old Roman road between Whitchurch and Warrington. There has probably been a church here since Saxon times and the Abbots of Vale Royal certainly maintained a prison at Weaverham, to suppress the rebellious peasantry.

A court was also held in the village, and the bailiff was kept busy with transgressors against monastic tyranny. One record tells of a fracas when the disaffected tenantry waylaid the abbot, leading to the arrest of many of them by Henry Done, the Master Forester of Delamere. Some of the trouble-makers were put into the stocks at Weaverham, and others in the prison, to await the abbot's pleasure.

In the time of Elizabeth I, Weaverham and its church were described as the worst in the province of York, with a vicar who was a 'common drunkard' and who had been found inebriated in a ditch more than once.

During the Civil Wars, Sir Thomas Aston and his lawless

troops plundered Weaverham and 'carried old men out of their houses, bound them together, tied them to a cart and drove them through mire and water to the dungeon'.

Piracy on the high seas later caused great excitement in Weaverham when Captain Hatton, who lived at Belle Vue House, turned out not to be the respected merchant trader that fellow 'Russets' thought.

Villagers could hardly believe their ears when word came of his appearance in court to answer charges of piracy. He was found guilty and sentenced to hang.

The Captain was, however, a clever man and arranged with a silver-smith for a special silver tube to be made which fitted snugly into his throat.

On the gallows he was asked if he had any last request, but silently shook his head and did the same when asked if there was any last word he would like to pass to his friends.

The hangman pulled the lever, the trap door opened and the Captain fell through. It was the law that a body had to hang for half an hour, and then it was cut down and given to friends for burial.

So it was with the Captain and a solemn undertaker placed him in his coffin for his friends to collect from the prison. When they arrived the Captain was sitting on his coffin... alive and well!

Justice had been done and the law carried out. He was a free man!

As a result, the law was promptly changed to ensure that never again would anyone cheat the hangman's noose and the words were added to the law, 'hanged by the neck UNTIL DEAD'.

Weaverham, at the beginning of the 20th century, had a far more romantic tale... the Hefferston Grange Elopement!

Hefferston Grange, on the outskirts of the village, was owned by Squire Heath, a bachelor and flamboyant member of the hunting set. In 1869, when he was 54, he met and married a beautiful young woman, Elizabeth Gooday, and together they had three daughters.

The youngest of these was Robina who was constantly in trouble with her father for her associations with village lads. One young suitor was Arthur Tomkinson, a stable lad who lived with his parents in a small cottage in Weaverham High Street. Arthur's father was a waggoner, employed on the Hefferston estate and it is not difficult to imagine what the old Squire thought of his daughter's relationship. The Squire died in 1907 and left his widow to sort out Robina's waywardness.

One night, Arthur made his way to the Grange where Robina was waiting at her bedroom window. He placed a ladder up to the window and together they made their way to Manchester where eventually, in April 1908, they were married. Later they returned to Arthur's parents' cottage, but the distress and scandal of the elopement persuaded Elizabeth Heath to put the estate up for sale.

It was assumed, quite wrongly, that Robina must have been pregnant to cause her to elope with Arthur and one village wit composed a long poem about the affair. One verse went:

Robina, Robina, I say have you seen her?
My darling she seems very shy.
If it's a daughter we'll wet it with porter,
If a boy we'll wet it with beer.

Despite their different backgrounds, the odds stacked against them, and the village gossips, Robina and Arthur remained together and had two children, but not until some years after the 'affair'.

Ships of The Forest

Nunsmere Hall, set in the rolling pasturelands of modern day Oakmere, is a plush country hotel, once the setting for a storyline in the UK's favourite television soap, Coronation Street, and the rural idyll chosen by former Prime Minister, Lady Thatcher, when she wished to complete, in solitude, her famous memoirs.

What Nunsmere Hall conceals is a past entwined with England's maritime history, some of the great ships of the 20th century and a rather fitting revival of Delamere Forest's links with the old sailing vessels of long ago.

Nunsmere Hall was built around 1900 for Sir Aubrey Brocklebank, Chairman of the famous Brocklebank Shipping Line, whose origins can be traced back to Cumberland in the 1700s.

From here, Sir Aubrey's ancestors sailed the seven seas and in 1770 they established a shipbuilding yard in New England. The American War of Independence brought that particular venture to an abrupt halt, but still the Brocklebanks prospered and in

Nunsmere Hall served as a hospital
in the First World War.

1820 they opened offices in the bustling port of Liverpool.

Soon the fleet began expanding to ply the world, from Calcutta and Bombay to Shangai and Lima.

Conversion to steam brought a new era and in 1911 Sir Aubrey became chairman of the Brocklebank Line which later played a vital role, at heavy cost, in maintaining the nation's food supplies during the First World War. By this time the company had already tentatively linked with Cunard, although it was a further twenty-five years before a merger was formally ratified, to bring about formation of the Cunard-Brocklebank Line.

Sir Aubrey became an influential director of Cunard in the 1920s and he was charged with drawing specifications and designs for a magnificent new liner which was to restore Cunard's fortunes in the trans-Atlantic passenger race.

At Nunsmere Hall, he mused over the plans of 7,000 experiments and no less than sixteen different models which were built and floated, under his personal direction, in a tank simulator. In the end he recommended a vast ship of approximately 1,000 ft. overall length, with a beam of 119 ft. and 81,000 gross tonnage.

This came to be the world famous Queen Mary, launched in 1934, though sadly, Sir Aubrey did not live to see 'his creation'.

Lady Brocklebank and her second son John remained at Nunsmere Hall until the Second World War when the building became a temporary hospital for the duration of hostilities. It later survived a chequered history and was eventually converted into a hotel, in the mid-1980s.

Upon the death of his elder brother, John Brocklebank, who had grown up at Nunsmere Hall, inherited the family title in 1953 and some years later reluctantly accepted the chairmanship of Cunard. In 1963, and through his prompting, a new Cunard 'Queen' was on the drawing board. This was to become the QE2.

Fall of the House of Egerton

Oulton Hall, early in the 20th century.

Beyond Cheshire, the best known corner of Old Delamere Forest is, unquestionably, the motor racing circuit of Oulton Park which, since 1953, has annually attracted thousands of enthusiasts to the otherwise secluded village of Little Budworth.

During the past half century some of the greatest names in motor sport have graced Oulton Park, from Stirling Moss, Mike Hawthorn and Geoff Duke to John Surtees, Jim Clark and Graham Hill.

Yet behind the twists and turns of the famous circuit lies an incredibly tragic story, 'The Fall of the House of Egerton'.

The family's antecedents were already chiselled into the backbone of Cheshire when, in the late 15th century, Sir John Egerton inherited lands at Oulton, by virtue of his marriage to a daughter of the Dones of Delamere Forest.

Thirty or so years later, on a slightly elevated site not far from the ancient church of Little Budworth, the Egertons erected a moated Tudor house which, during the Civil War siege of Chester, 1644, became a strategic outpost, garrisoned by Sir William Brereton, the Parliamentary commander in Cheshire.

Later, and whilst the fortunes of Kings and Parliament ebbed and flowed, the Egertons grew in wealth, power and standing, so that in 1715 a new, stately mansion was built, to designs by Sir John Vanbrugh, the designer of Blenheim Palace.

Successive Egertons (Grey-Egertons they became later) spent lavishly on Oulton Hall and its parkland and for many years it outshone even Tatton Hall, the home of their illustrious cousins at Rostherne. Priceless masterpieces and exotic taspestries adorned the walls of the 40-room mansion and externally, a veritable fortune was expended on landscaping 315 acres of parkland, the main features of which were a curved serpentine lake and a Catherine-wheel of tree-lined paths, all leading to the magnificent centrepiece of Oulton Hall.

It was into these splendid surroundings that Sir Philip Grey-Egerton moved with his young bride, a Baltimore belle, following their marriage in 1893. Two years later Mary, 'Mae', Grey-Egerton gave birth to twin sons, Philip and Rowland and they were christened at Little Budworth parish church.

The family succession was assured and villagers lined the lanes to welcome 'an heir and a spare'. The Oulton estate was secure, their homes and jobs secure.

Yet it was not to be. Sir Philip and his wife divorced and the drums of war could be heard in the distance.

On August 4th, 1914 the First World War began and Rowland Grey-Egerton was gazetted to the 2nd Battalion Royal Welsh Fusiliers. Promoted to Captain, he was killed after just twenty-two days active service in Flanders. Philip, his brother, survived the carnage of the Western Front and in 1918 when his health gave way he was sent home, to Oulton, to recuperate. In October, however, he was summoned to rejoin to his regiment and despite his father's pleadings, he insisted it was 'his duty' to return.

Within days he was in the Second Battle of Cambrai, part of

the British advance on the retreating Germans. On October 8th Philip perished during an ill-conceived, some might say 'mindless' cavalry charge on an impregnable German position.

Captain Philip, the last of the direct line of his family, lay dead amidst the mud and guts of a French battlefield.

Sir Philip Grey-Egerton was heartbroken and not many years after the Armistice he leased Oulton to the managing director of the Partington Steel & Iron Works.

On St Valentine's Day, 1926, the Egerton curse struck again.

It was a Sunday morning, bright and clear, when a footman spotted smoke rising from the roof of Oulton Hall. Fire brigades from Tarporley, Winsford and Chester raced to the scene, but upon arrival the place was an inferno.

Twenty people entered the hall to attempt to retrieve paintings, furniture and personal effects, but as they did so the roof timbers collapsed, bringing down a 30,000 gallon lead water tank.

The head maid, an auxiliary maid, and two young male servants perished instantly. The head gardener and a Tarporley fire officer died later in hospital as a result of their terrible burns.

Sir Philip died in 1937 and the destruction of the once magnificent hall was completed in 1940, by two bombs from a

German aircraft, 'unloading' after a raid over Liverpool.

Soon Oulton Park, commandeered for the war effort, had a 'new family', of thousands of soldiers, of many nationalities, but mainly Americans during the latter years of the Second World War. A network of roads around the camp was constructed and in the early 1950s, members of the Mid Cheshire Motor Club spied their chance to create a motor-racing circuit.

The first meeting, a 'private' event, took place on Saturday August 8th, 1953 and three months later, 40,000 people turned up for the inaugural first ever public motor-racing at Oulton Park.

A memorial service amidst the charred remains of the once magnificent Oulton Hall.

Forest Ways

The 'Switchback', in the 1920s. This is the local name for Ashton Road, between Hatchmere and Mouldsworth.

Drink and be merry!

Inns, pubs and beerhouses have always had their place in Delamere Forest, and in the immediate vicinity of the modern Linmere Visitor Centre there are still plenty to choose from, many with evocative names and histories all of their own.

The Abbey Arms (Oakmere), the Swan (Tarporley), and the Bluecap (Sandiway), have been mentioned earlier, but what of the Tiger's Head, Norley, the Carrier's Rest, Hatchmere, the Goshawk, Mouldsworth, the Forest View, Oakmere, the Hare & Hounds, Crowton, the Hanging Gate, Weaverham, the Robin Hood, Helsby, the Royal Oak, Kelsall?

All have long associations with Delamere Forest, though there can be few pubs, anywhere, with such a curious title as the 'Cabbage Hall', the wayside hostelry on the A49, at Oakmere.

An old 'beerhouse' originally stood on the site and was once a meeting place for salt smugglers evading tax during the Napoleonic Wars. Workers from Winsford would exchange salt for beer and then the precious commodity would be carried away on packhorses to foil the customs men.

The name 'Cabbage' Hall has nothing whatsoever to do with the vegetable. It appears from the late 19th century when the pub was owned by a tailor who, when making a suit to order, would save cut-off pieces of material to his own advantage. This proce-dure was known as 'cabbaging' and was how the tailor, 'Cabbage' Walker, supposedly raised the money to buy the pub!

CABBAGE HALL

About a mile south of the Cabbage Hall is the Fox & Barrel whose previous name was the King's Head. It was changed when a fox,

77

being hunted through the forest, made a dash for the cellar where it hid, behind a beer barrel. Reynard escaped and ever since the pub has been known as the Fox & Barrel. The pub is sited on the line of an ancient saltway that ran from Winsford to Chester.

At Cotebrook, also on the A49, is the Alvanley Arms, named after the once powerful Lords Alvanley who owned extensive lands in the area.

Rebuilt in 1648, it is a former coaching inn and served some of the many stagecoaches that passed by on the north-south highway linking Warrington and the north with Shrewsbury and the south.

In the 18th century it took three days and two nights to journey by stage from the Red Lion, Warrington, to the Bull Inn, London. A timetable of 1808 shows the Mail Coach, from

Toll Bar Cottage, Oakmere, looking along the A556 towards Northwich. The cottage was demolished in the 1930s and, today, is the site of the Shell service station.

Chester to York, stopping at 'Crabtree Green after crossing through Delamere Forest, via Kelsall', and puts the cost of a letter from Northwich to London at ten pence.

Norley

In medieval times, much of life in the village of Norley (the 'north clearing') revolved around the forest and its harsh laws and, according to legend, it was a retreat for outlaws, one of whom actually fled to join Robin Hood's band, in Sherwood Forest! On Gallowsclough Hill, poachers were supposedly hanged, after saying a prayer at Gadsbank (God's Bank). Nearby is Archery Field and the village pub, the Tiger's Head. Originally a 17th century farmhouse, it opened as a beerhouse in 1840, but to this day no-one can say how it came to have such an unusual name.

Barrow

The village of Barrow, made up of Great Barrow and Little Barrow, was at the southern extremity of the old forest, about four miles from Chester. Barrowmore Hall, built 1879/81 for Hugh Lyle Smyth, of Liverpool, became the East Lancashire Tuburculosis Colony in 1920. The sanatorium was completely destroyed by a landmine in 1940, resulting in the deaths of thirty-two patients and staff. Later Barrowmore Hospital was developed here.

In the old forest district of Kingswood, two other hospitals were built for the treatment of tuberculosis, a complaint prevalent in industrial cities. Fresh air treatment was the only known method of combatting the disease and the invigorating, clean air of the forest was considered ideal at the turn of the 20th century.

The Liverpool Sanatoria opened in 1901. It was set in forty acres, could house forty-nine patients and was paid for by the National Society for the Prevention of Tuberculosis. Two years later, the Manchester Sanatorium, known as Crossley, opened its doors to one-hundred patients. It was paid for by the Manchester industrialist, Sir William Crossley. Both buildings are now in private ownership.

Helsby Quarries

Stone from Helsby quarries was used to build the churches of Ince, Upton and Saltney, and for repairs to Chester Cathedral. Large quantities were also taken to build Liverpool & Birkenhead Docks and the Liverpool Customs House. A 'railway' track, laid across the marshes, made it possible to ship the stone direct to Liverpool.

Radio Masts

The British Telecom Radio Masts, on Pale Heights, are 560ft above sea level and are at one of the highest points on the Sandstone Ridge. The masts provide a high capacity radio-relay link, for Dublin, Chester, Liverpool and Manchester, to carry television signals and thousands of telephone circuits.

High Billinge

The clump of trees above Utkinton which may be seen for miles around is known as High Billinge where once stood a Bronze

Oakmere Hall, standing near to the crossroads of the A49 and the A556, is often referred to as a 'fairytale castle'. Its building, as a private residence, began in 1867/68, to designs by the celebrated Cheshire architect, John Douglas.

Age fort. When settlers left Liverpool bound for the New World, the last thing they reputedly saw of the old land was High Billinge.

Blakemere Hall
Built in the late 19th century, Blakemere Hall stood near to Sandiway and its former outbuildings are now the hub of the Blakemere Craft Centre.

Lord Barclay Paget lived here and then, prior to the First World War, Blakemere Hall was home to Walter Jones, an eccentric millionaire. The Prince of Wales, Edward VII, attended some of the grand parties here, but always insisted on travelling incognito, as 'Mr Peters'. Walter Jones enjoyed the sporting life, if not the exercise associated with it, and so devised a novel way of practising his shooting, without leaving his armchair! He had made a wooden model of a deer, on castors, and this his unfortunate butler had to pull around the grounds, so the master could take pot-shots at it!

During the Second World War, Blakemere Hall was utilised as a giant bakehouse, for the thousands of American soldiers who massed in the area prior to D-Day. The hall was pulled down after the war.

'Queen of the Forest'

In the 1860/70s Delamere Forest had its own miniature railway system. It was 2ft-7ins gauge and was used to carry marl for spreading on thousands of acres of land under clearance for agriculture. The little locomotive pulled up to sixty trucks and was known as the 'Queen of the Forest'.

Kelsborrow Castle

Kelsborrow Castle was an Iron Age promontory fort, above the hamlet of Willington, overlooking what is now the expanding village of Kelsall. It was home to people of the peace-loving Cornovii tribe who were easily subdued by the Romans. Now on private land, beyond Gooseberry Lane, it is a protected site. After the 1860s, with the coming of the railway, Willington was known as 'Little Switzerland', an attraction for 'tourists' from the cities who came to climb the hills, walk the quiet lanes and take a breath of Cheshire air. The local pub is the Boot Inn, known previously as 'The Cat', an unpleasant reminder of an occasion when a live cat was thrown on the fire for a bet!

Squatters Rights

Dwellings, 'built in a night', would occasionally spring up on the wastes and commons at the edge of Delamere Forest, their occupants claiming ancient 'Squatters Rights'. If the foresters allowed their vigilance to falter, and a crude dwelling was emitting smoke from a chimney by sunrise, there was nothing, legally, they could do about it. The dwelling would be enclosed in as much land as the builder could cover by throwing an axe from his door, in various directions.

Some of these properties, with their origins in the old practice, remain in the 21st century. The Image House, Bunbury, is one. It was erected by the notoroious poacher, Seth Shone, upon his

Delamere Station, staff and passengers, around 1905. The line was constructed by the West Cheshire Railway and opened in 1869.

return from transportation to Botany Bay. In one night he fashioned a great trunk of oak into a rafter and built his house around it, complete with kitchen chimney for the smoke. The next morning, with gun under arm, he paced his boundaries, saying that any who sought to hinder him would want but six feet of Bunbury churchyard! And when he had finished building, he carved images of the squire and his men and set them around the exterior, as a curse on those who had passed sentence upon him.

Forest Justice

The Master Foresters exercised their stranglehold on Delamere Forest's fifty townships by way of dungeons and courts, though not a single vestige remains. In the 19th century, modern police courts, the Eddisbury Petty Sessions, were held in the Abbey Arms pub until the Oakmere Courthouse was erected and opened in 1873. Now in a dilapidated condition, this building stands next to the Fourways Inn, on the A556. There were also gaols and lock-ups, in Kelsall, Bunbury, Tarporley and Over.

Little Budworth

Here is the motor racing circuit of Oulton Park. Until the 1800s it was called 'Budworth-le-Frith', whilst Oulton was known as 'Ferneleghes', the ferny clearings. These names of the great Forest of Delamere and one of the last, unclaimed, unfarmed vestiges of those long gone days is the ancient wasteland, Little Budworth Common.